# LOOKING AT PAINTINGS

# Dogs

*Dog*, 1967
Wayne Thiebaud, American, born 1920

# Dogs

Peggy Roalf

Series Editor
Jacques Lowe

Designer
Joseph Guglietti

Hyperion Books for Children
New York

Printed in Italy

FIRST EDITION

1  3  5  7  9  10  8  6  4  2

ISBN 1-56282-530-5 (trade)/1-56282-531-3 (lib.bdg.)

Original design concept by Amy Hill

# Contents

Introduction 7

*HUNTING SCENE*
Unknown Spanish artist 8

*PUPPY CARRYING A PHEASANT FEATHER*
Yi Om 10

*GIAN FEDERICO MADRUZZO*
Giovanni Battista Moroni 12

*THE ANIMALS ENTERING NOAH'S ARK*
Jacopo Bassano 14

*PLATO GIVES ADVICE TO ISKANDAR*
Attributed to Basawan 16

*PRINCE FERDINAND VI*
Jean Ranc 18

*WHITE POODLE IN A PUNT*
George Stubbs 20

*PORTRAIT OF AN EXTRAORDINARY MUSICAL DOG*
Philip Reinagle 22

*A DOG*
Francisco de Goya y Lucientes 24

*PIERREPONT EDWARD LACEY AND HIS DOG, GUN*
Noah North 26

*GROUP OF ARTISTS*
Marie Laurencin 28

*IN THE RAIN*
Franz Marc 30

*THE ROOF PLAYGROUND*
William Zorach 32

*CAPE COD EVENING*
Edward Hopper 34

*MAN LEADING DOG*
Bill Traylor 36

*SUNNY*
Alex Katz 38

*COUNTRY DOG GENTLEMEN*
Roy De Forest 40

*STEPPING OUT*
Gilbert Sánchez Luján 42

*FLYING YELLOW DOG*
Grimanessa Amoros 44

Glossary and Index 46

Credits 48

*To my mother, with love*

# Introduction

*LOOKING AT PAINTINGS* is a series of books about understanding what great artists see and think about when they paint. Dogs and people have formed close bonds since prehistoric times, when hunting and guard dogs were essential to human survival. Throughout history, painters have portrayed this animal's loyalty and affection with spirited insight.

An anonymous twelfth-century artist depicted a trio of hunting dogs as expressive silhouettes to symbolize the animals' speed and keen instincts. The Korean artist Yi Om painted an adorable puppy as a religious emblem to ward off thieves and wrongdoers. This loving portrayal conveys the personal relationship Korean people had with their religious rituals.

The canine's unquestioning loyalty inspired Francisco de Goya y Lucientes's tragic picture of an abandoned dog. Painted in the 1820s, this scene, in which a sad little dog yearns after the shadow of its vanished master, suggests the end of the world. Contemporary artist Roy De Forest expressed the dog's instinctive ability to distinguish good from bad people. His dogs live in their own Garden of Eden, a happy world ruled by kindness and joy.

The amusing qualities of dogs inspired eighteenth-century painter George Stubbs to portray a poodle caught during a moment of dreadful uncertainty. With sympathy, Stubbs conveyed the humor in this dog's embarrassment. In 1986, Gilbert Sánchez Luján depicted a character rooted in Chicano folklore as a sly dog that pokes fun at human vanity. Through his clear, graphic style, Sánchez created a figure reminiscent of the class clown in everybody's childhood.

Great artists have transformed their love of dogs into majestic and fanciful images. By seeing how they have portrayed dogs, you can learn to observe your own cherished pet with the eyes of a painter.

*HUNTING SCENE,*  detail, 12th century
Unknown Spanish artist, fresco transferred to canvas, 114³⁄₁₆" x 52³⁄₄"

These hounds giving chase to their quarry were originally painted on a wall in the San Baudilio Monastery in Berlanga, Spain. Using simple materials and a limited *palette*, an anonymous twelfth-century artist created a *fresco* alive with movement and grace.

When this painting was created, paper was not readily available, so the artist designed the *mural* directly on the wall that was to be painted. First, he drew the scene in *charcoal*, carefully designing the spaces between the dogs to give their silhouetted forms a feeling of movement. When he was happy with the *composition*, he painted over the charcoal lines with *watercolor*, dusted away the charcoal marks with a bouquet of feathers, and completed the mural with paint.

The muralist echoed a feeling of movement conveyed by the dogs' pointed noses in the spiky, upturned branches of the trees.

By the 1950s, the painting was in bad condition, nearly ruined by water damage. A team of conservators, specialists who restore damaged works of art, transferred the mural from the wall onto *canvas*. First, a piece of canvas was coated with an extremely tacky glue and applied to the painting. With a sharp knife, a cut was made along all four sides of the picture through both the canvas and the top layer of *plaster* to separate the mural from the surrounding wall. The canvas was then carefully peeled away, taking with it the entire painting, which adhered to the glue on the canvas. Because the scene was reversed, as though seen in a mirror, the process was repeated to transfer the mural onto a second piece of canvas.

This beautiful painting was saved using a conservation method first perfected in the eighteenth century. This method has since been used to save countless murals from destruction caused by time, floods, and pollution.

8

*PUPPY CARRYING A PHEASANT FEATHER*, 16th century
Yi Om, Korean (1499–unknown), watercolor on silk, 12¼" x 17¼"

During the fifteenth century, Korean painters adopted the materials, the methods, and the styles of Chinese artists, their northern neighbors. They breathed new life into the formal style of Chinese art, which was based on strict ethical and religious beliefs. Because Buddhist ceremonies in Korea were an intimate part of family life, paintings created for daily rituals had a warm informal quality that expressed a more personal relationship between people and their religion.

Yi Om specialized in animal paintings that were used to ward off evil. His painting of an adorable puppy symbolized a guard dog's ability to protect a family from thieves. This wonderful combination of affection and humor served to charm wrongdoers away, rather than to frighten them.

Working on silk, Yi painted each *line* and every *shade* of color with single brushstrokes. He first drew the puppy and feather in outline and then applied a tan color to the entire *drawing*. He shaped the body with russet, leaving areas of tan uncovered to form the dog's quizzical face and the delicate markings on the feather. While the silk was still damp, Yi added a darker shade of russet to the paws. The moist silk absorbed the wet paint, creating the soft velvety effect of puppy fur. Yi had to work quickly and masterfully, for once his colors touched the absorbent silk, the marks were permanent and could not be changed.

Yi gave this picture the special qualities that mark traditional Korean painting. He took an original view of a familiar subject and created a playful image designed to amuse the viewer and, therefore, refresh his or her spirit.

*I. Herring, a nineteenth-century American, first drew these puppies on a stone, using a greasy crayon. He then inked the stone and made impressions on paper, creating prints called lithographs.*

10

*GIAN FEDERICO MADRUZZO,* about 1560
Giovanni Battista Moroni, Italian (about 1525–78), oil on canvas, 79 ½" x 46"

Giovanni Battista Moroni lived in the remote fortified town of Bergamo, Italy, in the 1500s and established a successful career painting *portraits.* Moroni's *patrons* were his fellow townspeople: church officials, aristocrats, and local businessmen.

Gian Federico Madruzzo was a cardinal of the Catholic church, the highest-ranking priest in the region. Moroni depicted this important member of the community as an unpretentious, seemingly ordinary man. Through the sophisticated *composition,* however, Moroni captured Madruzzo's spiritual greatness.

Moroni expressed this miniature spaniel's love for its master through its sweet expression.

Moroni made the cardinal seem larger than life through the *contrast* in size between the man and his miniature pet dog. The tall narrow shape of the *canvas,* the vertical *forms* in the *background,* and the black fur lining of Madruzzo's robe intensify this effect. Posing the little spaniel next to Madruzzo's enormous foot, Moroni further emphasized the cardinal's stature.

Moroni captured the dog's glossy coat using a combination of *opaque* and *transparent* paint. He formed the markings in thick white paint and the darker areas in russet diluted with *turpentine.* When that layer was dry, he applied an even film of pale yellow, creating a warm overall *tone.* With delicate strokes of greenish gray, he then fashioned the edges of the dog's coat into feathery strands. The dog's sweet face and relaxed body form an amusing contrast with the cardinal's serious expression and wooden pose.

By including the cardinal's pet dog, Moroni gave this subdued yet surprising portrait a special meaning. He suggests that Cardinal Madruzzo was a true shepherd of his congregation.

*THE ANIMALS ENTERING NOAH'S ARK,* detail, date unknown
Jacopo Bassano, Italian (1517–92), oil on canvas, 81½" x 104⅛"

*J*acopo Bassano lived in a rural town forty miles from Venice, a distance which, during the sixteenth century, was more than a day's journey. He viewed life in a different way than urban painters who were routinely influenced by politics and church business. Bassano's more famous contemporaries, Titian and Paolo Veronese, glorified their *patrons* in scenes of people controlling nature, whereas Bassano portrayed people as an integral part of the natural world.

Bassano made the biblical story of Noah and the great Flood seem like an event that had taken place in his own backyard. He painted the local landscape, and he depicted the biblical figures wearing contemporary clothes. Bassano expressed his fondness and respect for dogs by including five handsome canines among the pairs of other animals. Alone among the creatures waiting their turn to board the ark, the dogs reveal personality and intelligence. Bassano captured a dog's awareness of the impending disaster in the eyes of a spaniel huddled at its mate's feet.

Bassano used the technique of *perspective,* making the figures gradually smaller to create a realistic sense of depth. In the *foreground,* the large figure of Noah stands above the throng of animals. In the middle, a small russet dog on the ramp seems dwarfed by the enormous ark. A covey of birds frames the *background* where a flock of tiny sheep makes the pasture seem far away.

Bassano's artistic vision was so unusual in his time that many Venetians, including Titian, eagerly collected his scenes of people and animals in luminous landscape settings.

*Bassano used atmospheric perspective to create a sense of depth, making the colors gradually lighter as they become more distant.*

*PLATO GIVES ADVICE TO ISKANDAR,* detail, 1597–98
Attributed to Basawan, ink, colors, and gold on paper, 9⅞" x 6¼"

*A*kbar the Great was a sixteenth-century philosopher-king who ruled the Mogul empire in what is today part of northern India and Pakistan. Akbar established a studio in which more than one hundred painters created one-of-a-kind albums of classic Islamic literature called *illuminated manuscripts*. The painter Basawan illustrated a poem by the thirteenth-century author Amir Khusrau. In this scene, a falconer and a pair of hunting dogs sniffing their quarry lead us into an ideal world painted in miniature.

Basawan chose a view from high above and spread the people, animals, and plants across the open area so that each can be clearly seen. Although the figures are all painted at the same *scale*, Basawan created a feeling of depth through their placement on the page. The dogs and hunters at the bottom seem nearer, whereas the figures closer to the top seem distant. Basawan emphasized this effect by having the figures in the *foreground* standing and those in the middle crouching or sitting.

Basawan defined the *contours* of the figures and the rocky terrain with delicate *shading*, but to evoke a timeless feeling, he deliberately avoided the use of *shadows*. Basawan animated his portrayals of the dogs and people through expressive gestures and details. These he first drew in ink, then painted in *watercolor*, using pigments mined from the earth: ocher, umber, zinc white, and minium red, from which the term "miniature painting" takes its name.

Unlike most of the painters in Akbar's studio, who remained anonymous, Basawan became a legend because he made even inanimate objects, such as rocks, look as if they had life.

*Amir Khusrau's poem was inscribed in calligraphy, or beautiful writing, on luminous gold leaf.*

*PRINCE FERDINAND VI,* about 1725
Jean Ranc, French (1674–1735), oil on canvas, 56⅝" x 45⅝"

Jean Ranc received his training at the Royal Academy of Painting and Sculpture in Paris. In 1724, he was appointed first painter to King Philip V of Spain, the grandson of King Louis XIV of France. Philip infused the Spanish court with an elegant French style, bringing painters, musicians, and *artisans* from Paris to his palace in Madrid.

For this jewellike *portrait* of Philip's son Ferdinand and his playful greyhound, Ranc first created the painting in grisaille, a French art term meaning "shades of gray." He began by coating a *canvas* with light gray paint. Using *opaque* white, he formed the areas that would be the lightest in the finished painting, including the dog's white markings and the boy's skin. Ranc shaped the medium and dark tones in gray and then allowed the painting to dry completely.

*For this drawing of a greyhound, Albrecht Dürer (1471–1528) held his brush close to the bristles to carefully control the movement of the brush and, therefore, the flow of ink.*

When Ranc was satisfied with every aspect of the *composition*, including the placement of the boy and his dog and the range of dark, medium, and light tones, he applied thin veils of color called *glazes*. To create the dog's gleaming coat, he painted a glaze of silvery blue, wiping most of the color off with a cloth to produce a soft glow. The original gray-and-white painting shows through, forming the dog's markings and the subtle *shading* and *highlights*. After applying glazes throughout, Ranc used fine brushes and opaque colors to create a brilliant highlight on the greyhound's eye and the richly *detailed* embroidery on the prince's jacket and stockings.

Due to the painstaking method of grisaille and glazing, this portrait remains as brilliant and unmarred by cracks as it was the day that Ranc signed his name.

*WHITE POODLE IN A PUNT,* about 1780
George Stubbs, English (1724–1806), oil on canvas, 50" x 40"

Through self-education, George Stubbs developed a rare talent for painting animals. He studied briefly with an artist who required his students to copy paintings from books. Stubbs, who preferred painting live subjects, left to work on his own. He also studied anatomy with a local veterinarian in order to improve his skill in *drawing* animals.

Stubbs created this arresting *portrait* for a client who requested a painting of a favorite dog. This poodle, bred and trained to hunt in water, seems frightened by the motion of the boat and embarrassed by his lack of confidence.

Using fine brushes, Stubbs created a wide variety of *textures*. He blended a range of pale colors, from rose and gold *hues* to brilliant whites, to form the dog's dense curly coat, shiny nose, and moist eyes. He created a solid, three-dimensional feeling through the light green *shading* that mirrors the colors of the trees reflected in the water.

The idyllic landscape forms an unusual *contrast* with the cowering dog. Stubbs first painted the trees and the water in reddish brown, like the boat. Over this, he shaped the weeping willows and the marsh grass in green and ocher, and the water in blue. The touches of green, rose, and yellow in the dog echo the overall *tone* in the landscape that gives the painting a romantic feeling.

After his death, Stubbs and his work were almost forgotten until the 1930s, when renewed interest in animal painting restored him to his proper place among the masters.

*The English painter Thomas Gainsborough (1727–88) emphasized a mother dog's natural protective instincts through the wild rocky setting.*

*PORTRAIT OF AN EXTRAORDINARY MUSICAL DOG,* about 1805
Philip Reinagle, English (1749–1833), oil on canvas, 28 ¼" x 36 ½"

Philip Reinagle began his career as a *portrait* artist and later made animal painting his specialty. His *patrons* were wealthy people who lived in rural England during the nineteenth century and *commissioned* portraits of their favorite animals to decorate their houses. In 1803, Reinagle published a book featuring twenty-four pictures of hunting dogs, which became a standard reference for English painters of animals.

Reinagle's remarkable painting of a musically gifted spaniel invites the imagination to run wild, for nobody knows why or for whom it was made. He created a *dynamic composition* free of distracting objects. Through the slanting *lines* in the piano that meet the vertical lines of the window frame, Reinagle focuses attention on the dog. The bright white sheet music at a sharp angle to the piano separates the animal from the soft *shadows* in the *background.*

In 1815, the French painter Théodore Géricault personified England as a fierce bulldog to signify the animosity between that country and his homeland, which had been at war for ten years.

Reinagle gave the spaniel a lifelike presence through his virtuoso brushwork and an *oil* painting technique called fat over lean. First, he painted the dog in brown paint thinned with *turpentine,* emphasizing the darkest shadows. After the thin, or lean, layer had dried, he applied the lighter russet and golden tones with paint thickened, or fattened, with oil. Finally, he created sparkling *highlights* in the eyes and on the collar with *opaque* white paint. By building up the colors in gradually thicker layers that were permitted to dry between work sessions, Reinagle ensured that the paint would not crack with age.

With this canine prodigy, Reinagle gave an amusing twist to the art term "conversation piece"—a painting of people with their children and favorite animals designed to delight the viewer and stimulate conversation.

*A DOG*, about 1820–23
Francisco de Goya y Lucientes, Spanish (1746–1828), mural transferred to canvas, 53½" x 32"

After a lifetime of working to achieve fame and wealth as the official painter to the kings of Spain, Francisco de Goya y Lucientes abandoned Madrid and his official duties in 1819. The country was bankrupt and had lost its position as a European power due to the corrupt and tyrannical rule of King Ferdinand VII. Goya moved to a country estate, where he painted a series of *murals*. In these scenes, called Goya's Black Paintings, the artist expressed his struggle to maintain his spiritual faith, which had been badly shaken by the misery that engulfed his country.

The most tragic painting in the series depicts a mongrel dog alone in a nightmarish landscape. Goya made the creature seem lost and helpless through the *contrast* between the animal's small size and the enormous *scale* of the *background*. The dog looks longingly at a ghostly *shadow* that suggests his vanished human master.

Goya created this stark, emotional scene using simple methods. In the background, which suggests a world in flames, he applied thick layers of rose-, umber-, and rust-colored paint. He then painted blotches of chrome yellow and white, blending the colors together with large brushes. Goya emphasized the animal's struggle through the *foreground* that seems like a wall blocking the dog's escape. He formed the dog's head as a gray silhouette and conveyed its sorrowful expression through a few yellow *highlights* that reflect the raging inferno.

This dramatic painting has led many scholars to believe that it is a symbolic *self-portrait* expressing Goya's despair over the chaos that surrounded him.

*The German painter Philipp Otto Runge (1777–1810) created the expressive outlines of this baying dog with scissors, forming a paper cutout called a silhouette.*

*PIERREPONT EDWARD LACEY AND HIS DOG, GUN,* about 1835–36
Noah North, American (1809–80), oil on canvas, 42" x 30"

*A*ll that is known about Noah North's career as a *portrait* painter comes from public records and advertisements published during his lifetime. Journeying by horse and by canal barge, North roamed throughout the frontier region of western New York and as far as Columbus, Ohio, to create portraits of rural families. During the winter, when travel was difficult, North applied his artistic skills to practical work, such as decorative painting on signs, furniture, and carriages.

Like other self-taught folk artists', North's style evolved through working from close observation and from his hands-on knowledge. He posed Pierrepont Edward Lacey and his cherished mastiff, Gun, straight on to give the pair an imposing presence. North painted one of the dog's hind legs in the *background* to suggest depth. However, because he was not skilled in *perspective drawing*, North made the dog's rear leg as large as the front legs, rather than smaller, which would have created a feeling of distance from the viewer.

North created a variety of textures to convey the mastiff's soulful eyes; its soft, velvety muzzle; and its bristle-stiff whiskers.

Through careful study, North captured the dog's bright eyes, sleek coat, and soft muzzle. To convey Gun's solid stance, North fashioned the dog's legs like those of the furniture he decorated. With almost invisible brushstrokes, he depicted young Lacey's stylish green suit embellished with gold embroidery. Although the boy's features are clearly defined, the face we see is that of a young adult, rather than a child, for North was more experienced in portraying older people.

After his marriage in 1841, North turned his attention to farming, lumber manufacturing, and teaching in order to stay at home with his family. So far, no paintings by North dated after the 1840s have been discovered.

*GROUP OF ARTISTS,* 1908
Marie Laurencin, French (1883–1956), oil on canvas, 24¾" x 31⅛"

As a teenager, Marie Laurencin immersed herself in art, literature, and poetry, and she began to study painting seriously in 1903. Through her classmates at the Académie Humbert in Paris, she met Pablo Picasso, the Spanish painter who was revolutionizing modern art through his unusual ways of depicting people and objects. Four years later, she created this group *portrait* of her friends who often held parties at Picasso's studio: Picasso and his dog, Frika; the artist herself; her boyfriend, the poet Guillaume Apollinaire; and the painter Fernande Olivier, Picasso's girlfriend.

Like Picasso, Laurencin was inspired by African sculpture and tribal artifacts. In this painting, she simplified the portraits into masklike faces defined with bold outlines.

Laurencin gave the scene an air of formality through the dark clothes and *contrasting* areas of white in the dog and in the men's shirts. The strong triangular arrangement of the figures, with Apollinaire in the center and herself at the top, makes Laurencin and the poet the center of attention.

Using expressive black *lines,* Laurencin depicted unique aspects of each personality. Upturned lines shaping Frika's eye and mouth convey a mischievous puppylike personality. The double outline emphasizes Picasso's eye, suggesting his constant search for new ways to express his artistic vision. She captured Olivier's feminine gesture through the gentle curves shaping her head and arms. A *shadow* over half of her face gives Laurencin's *self-portrait* an air of mystery.

The original owner of this painting was the American author Gertrude Stein, who lived in Paris. Stein was the first to bring Laurencin's work to the attention of art collectors in the United States.

*In 1864, Rosa Bonheur created this Renaissance-style portrait of a working-class sheepdog, complete with traditional Roman lettering for its title.*

## IN THE RAIN, 1912

Franz Marc, German (1880–1916), oil on canvas, 31⅞" x 41½"

**F**ranz Marc became a painter after studying religion, philosophy, and languages. Until he met the Russian painter Wassily Kandinsky in 1911, Marc struggled to find his own point of view as an artist. Together, they founded an organization called The Blue Rider to develop a new form of art that explored spiritual, rather than material, aspects of life. With a new sense of purpose, Marc created a powerful body of work over the next five years.

Marc believed that animals living in nature had a special innocence that was unspoiled by people. He created this painting of a dog based on natural *forms*, but *abstracted* into simpler shapes. Marc depicted a primordial landscape that evokes the Garden of Eden. The rainfall conveys the symbolic use of water to purify, or baptize. In this ideal setting, a dog is blissfully at peace with the human race.

Marc composed the painting in a kaleidoscopic array of colors and slanted forms, which he called force *lines*, to express the positive energy of life. A rock outcrop on the right, painted in a series of angular shapes, focuses attention on the white dog in the *foreground*. A tree in the middle of the garden echoes the orange colors forming the woman and the face of the man in the center. Marc balanced the angular shapes with curved shapes in the dog, the foliage, and the woman's figure.

Painting was a vehicle through which Marc sought meaning in his life. His search was cut short with the outbreak of World War I in 1914, and ended two years later when he was killed on the battlefield at Verdun, France.

*Franz Marc painted this dog's features with simplified lines that suggest the animal's gentle innocence.*

*THE ROOF PLAYGROUND*, detail, 1917
William Zorach, American (1887–1966), oil on canvas, 29" x 23¾"

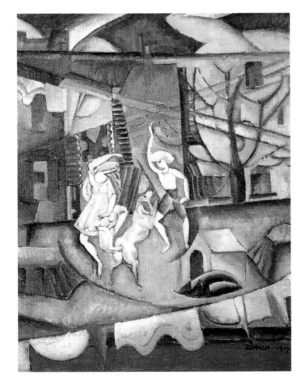

*The leafless tree in the background, painted flat like a stage set, emphasizes the theatrical quality of this playful scene.*

As a child William Zorach learned to never lose sight of his dreams. In 1910, he emigrated with his mother from Lithuania to Cleveland, Ohio, joining his father, who had earlier fled anti-Semitism. Although he often had to drop out of school to help support the family, young Zorach worked as a *commercial artist* and studied painting at night. In less than a year, he had saved enough money to continue his studies in New York and in Paris, France. There Zorach fell in love with Marguerite Thompson, another art student. They married in 1912, pursued their careers, and raised a family.

Back in New York City, Zorach observed a rooftop playground and transformed the hard-edged cityscape into a joyous little theater. Zorach depicted the neighbors' laundry as bannerlike decorations and suggested the edge of a stage through the crescent-shaped zones of color on the ground.

Zorach formed the *composition* with curved shapes and diagonal *lines* that give the painting a *dynamic* feeling of energy and fun. Two clotheslines that crisscross the scene make us feel that we are looking down on the scene from above. Zorach echoed the curving upturned lines of the children and their pet in the doghouse roof and the tree in the *background*. A series of slanting lines and the reddish rectangular building in the distance suggest a feeling of depth in the flatly painted scene.

The year that he created this picture, Zorach achieved his dream of becoming a successful painter. With new confidence, he began carving figures out of wood, and a few years later he was also acclaimed for his sculptures of children and of animals.

## CAPE COD EVENING, 1937
Edward Hopper, American (1882–1967), oil on canvas, 30¼" x 40¼"

*E*dward Hopper often found inspiration for his paintings in poetry. On an autumn day on Cape Cod, Massachusetts, he observed the pale afternoon light brighten momentarily before fading to dusk. In this scene, Hopper used the close of day as a metaphor for the end of summer and the onset of winter.

Hopper evokes a mood of loneliness through a couple who seem remote from each other. The woman stands in self-absorbed silence as the man tries to attract the attention of a collie who is fixated on a sound or a sight beyond the picture.

Hopper based this *composition* on real and imaginary people and places. In a neighboring town, he sketched a house with a tall, heavily carved doorway. The man and woman are composites of several people whose strong features impressed the artist. In his studio, Hopper referred to his sketches and drew from memory as he worked on the painting. He emphasized the theme of shared solitude through the placement of the three figures. They are physically apart but visually united by the *lines* of an invisible triangle.

Hopper emphasized the stark atmosphere through a limited *palette* of colors: white, blue, ocher, green, and burnt sienna. The *transparent* blue *shadows* on the house give the white siding a chilly feeling. The green *shading* on the grass, the tree trunks, and the dog evokes the cool, fading light.

*Contemporary painter Alex Colville emphasized the hound's powerful sense of smell through the angular pose, placing the dog's nose in the foreground of the picture.*

The spare simplicity of this scene belies the mental effort that the process of creating each painting required of Hopper. He wrote that he struggled to prevent the physical ease of painting from distracting him from his original idea, which was often a harsh vision of life.

*MAN LEADING DOG,* about 1939–42
Bill Traylor, American (1854–1947), poster paint and pencil on cardboard,
15 ¼" x 15 ⅛"

**B**ill Traylor grew up in slavery and was freed in 1866 after the Civil War. He became a painter at the age of eighty-four, when illness forced him to retire from his job in a factory. Traylor set up his studio on the sidewalk next to a fruit stand in Montgomery, Alabama. He created paintings on discarded pieces of cardboard, revealing an imaginary world populated by people and animals often engaged in contests of will.

Traylor made a humorous observation on the power of animals to dominate their masters in *Man Leading Dog.* The fierce canine has clearly taken control of the tiny man.

Traylor was a self-taught painter with a special gift for conveying personality through simplified but expressive *forms.* The curved and pointed *contour* of the dog's massive body suggests the animal's aggressive nature. The thin red *lines* of the harness, by *contrast,* emphasize its big powerful neck. The mouth bristling with spiky teeth seems to bark: Beware of dog.

Traylor created a feeling of movement through the arrangement of the two figures on the cardboard. By placing the man's and the animal's heads close to the edge, he formed the unpainted *background* into a series of large and small angular shapes pointing in different directions. Crisp lines in the leash, the harness, and the legs slant toward the right edge of the cardboard, emphasizing the pair's forward motion.

During his three years as an artist, Traylor created more than twelve hundred pictures, many of which he sold for the price of a meal. Today his paintings are treasured by people all over the world who recognize the child in Traylor that never grew old.

*SUNNY,* 1971
Alex Katz, American (born 1929), oil on canvas, 96" x 72"

When Alex Katz began his career in 1949, most successful painters in New York City were creating wall-size *abstract canvases*. Katz, however, was interested in *portrait* painting. In the 1960s, inspired by billboards, he began enlarging his portraits to enormous proportions. Katz worked in smooth, flat zones of color that depict a world much like the one we live in but untroubled by difficulties.

Katz's portrait of Sunny transforms a small Skye terrier into a monumental icon of canine charisma. In this eight-foot-high painting, Sunny, nose-deep in sea grass, revels in the great outdoors.

Katz created an idyllic setting through the tranquil blue water and the distant islands bathed in misty light. By painting a series of slanted *forms*—the dog's magnificent ears, the forest on the right, and the triangular patch of grass on the left—Katz gives this peaceful scene a *dynamic* feeling that conveys the pent-up energy of a city dog let loose in the wilderness.

Katz first blocked in the shape of Sunny's head, ears, and chest in a flatly painted area of gray. He simplified the dog's silky coat to ribbons of white paint, into which he blended touches of gray while the white was still wet. Katz defined the lower edges of the ears using green paint to shape the fringed silhouette. Then he added white *highlights* over the gray with soft feathery brushstrokes to convey Sunny's gleaming coat. The bright red tongue, fourteen inches long in actual size, focuses attention on the happy dog. Katz simplified the *foreground* in a series of carefully observed pale green marks that suggest tender shoots of grass.

Sunny, the cherished family pet, also appears in portraits by Katz of his wife, Ada, and their son Vincent.

## COUNTRY DOG GENTLEMEN, 1973
Roy De Forest, American (born 1930), polymer on canvas, 67" x 97"

*A*s a young artist, Roy De Forest was unhappy with the *abstract* painting fashionable in the 1950s and searched for a different way to express his ideas. Inspired by books about adventure and exploration, he created fantastic landscapes in which animals, the central characters, led people on imaginary journeys.

In *Country Dog Gentlemen*, De Forest created a world where wise and noble dogs, supercharged with canine powers, invite good people to share their own Garden of Eden. Like sentries, they guard a paradise filled with exotic plants in electric colors.

De Forest painted this scene in a crazy quilt of shapes, colors, and *textures*. The animals' eyes, depicted as gleaming kaleidoscopic *designs*, convey their penetrating ability to size up people. Purple shadows emphasize the shepherd's acute sense of hearing. A pattern of red dots beaming from the little black creature suggests the all-seeing, all-knowing nature of dogs.

De Forest, whose two dogs have the run of his studio, uses nontoxic *acrylic* paint. He also prefers acrylic to *oil* paint because more bright colors are available, and he can create a greater variety of textures by blending special additives into the paint. He combined a thick gel with the colors in the vegetation to create tendrils and globules that stand up from the surface. For the flat zones of yellow light, he diluted the paint with a watery fluid called an extender. Large and small overlapping shapes painted in smooth and textured colors suggest a feeling of depth.

The dogs that populate De Forest's paintings suggest a happy world ruled by kindness and joy.

*Using the flat side of a crayon as well as the pointed end, Milton Avery created gray tones and black marks that convey this terrier's wiry coat.*

## STEPPING OUT, 1986
Gilbert Sánchez Luján, American (born 1940), pastel on paper, 30" x 44"

Gilbert Sánchez Luján grew up in East Los Angeles during the 1950s. Rock and roll was the new sound in music, new freeways linked the sprawling suburbs, and gas was cheap. Young Chicanos created a culture defined by their obsession with cars and by the hip fashion attitude of Hollywood. Nightlife centered on the ritual of dressing up and showing off in slow-moving brightly painted cars called low riders.

In *Stepping Out*, Sánchez gently mocks vanity through the trickster, a whimsical character drawn from Chicano and American Indian folklore. Represented as a mischievous dog, the trickster pokes fun at his stylish human companion.

Sánchez suggested the mood and the character of the figures through expressive *lines* and *forms* rather than precise *details*. The outline of the man's head conveys the ultimate in trendy haircuts. The fur collar and jeweled pin evoke the fashionable dress of old-time Hollywood film tycoons. Sánchez created almost identical smiling mouths on the man and his dog, echoing the popular belief that people eventually resemble their pets.

Sánchez worked in pastel, a medium that suits his graphic style. Pastel is made of pigment ground into a fine powder and formed into a stick with a small amount of gluelike resin. Colors range from pale *tints* to brilliant *hues*. Sánchez first sketched in the figure with green lines. He created the dark tones by applying broad strokes of blue, black, and white side by side and blending them together with a soft piece of leather called chamois. He then emphasized the outlines using orange and white to create a neon effect.

The clarity of Sánchez's style makes this sly dog symbolic of the class clown in everybody's childhood.

*Using chalk sharpened to a fine point, Leonardo da Vinci (1452–1519) defined a dog's muscular form by drawing short parallel lines that follow the curves of its body.*

*FLYING YELLOW DOG*, 1985–93
Grimanessa Amoros, Peruvian (born 1962), acrylic and mixed media on
canvas, 38" x 40"

**W**hen Grimanessa Amoros was thirteen years old, her mother and father
gave her a dog that was hers alone to love and care for. When she argued
with her parents, Amoros had long conversations with her pet, Toffee, about
the difficulties of growing up. She yearned for independence but also loved
her family, so she struggled to be patient until she was old enough to leave
her home in Peru.

When Amoros began her career as a painter in New York at age twenty-two,
she often saw a neighbor walking a dog much like Toffee. Inspired by the dog's
vivacious spirit, Amoros created this painting, which recalls her childhood dreams
of escaping to a special world where she and Toffee could do what they pleased.

Amoros applied layer upon layer of acrylic paint to build up
a thick texture called impasto.

Amoros painted these interplanetary
voyagers using a combination of materials
to create the *textured* surface. She worked
over an old painting that she no longer
liked, which had thick applications of
paint on top of leaves she had glued onto
the *canvas*. Amoros began the new picture
by shaping the dog with black *acrylic*
paint. When the black had dried, she
brushed on white and brilliant *shades* of
yellow, allowing areas of black underneath to show through. Although this
scene has a spontaneous feeling, Amoros
developed the figures gradually, modifying the *contours* until she was happy
with the *composition*. Then she emphasized the outlines and gave the dog a
mischievous expression.

Amoros bartered this painting for several months' rent on her apartment.
Eight years later, she offered her landlord a different painting in exchange,
because *Flying Yellow Dog* reminded her of a special time in her life. Amoros
then added cerulean blue, making the *background* seem like a far-off galaxy.

# Glossary and Index

ABSTRACT, 30, 38, 40: Having form and color but not recognizable subject matter.

Amoros, Grimanessa, 44

*Animals Entering Noah's Ark, The*, 15

ARTISAN, 18: A skilled craftsman or craftswoman who creates decorative useful objects of artistic merit by hand.

BACKGROUND, 12, 14, 22, 24, 26, 32, 36, 44: The part of a painting behind the subject; the distant area. *See also* FOREGROUND

Basawan, 16

Bassano, Jacopo, 14

CANVAS, 8, 18, 44: A woven fabric (often linen or cotton) used as a painting surface. It is usually stretched tight and stapled onto a wooden frame in order to produce a flat, unwrinkled surface.

*Cape Cod Evening*, 35

CHARCOAL, 8: A soft, black stick of burned wood, used to make drawings. Painters use charcoal because it can be blended and smudged to produce lines and tones as in a painting, but in black and white.

COLOR, as it is used by painters, is identified by three different terms. The actual appearance of the color (red, blue, bluish green, etc.) is its *hue*. Everyday words can be used to describe a hue that occurs in nature, such as rose, sky blue, and grass green.

A lighter or darker version of a hue, created by adding white or black, is called a *shade*.

A hue that is changed by adding a small amount of another color is a *tint*. For example, a painter might add a small amount of red to gray, to yellow, and to blue and create reddish tints of these original colors.

COMMERCIAL ARTIST, 32: An artist who is commissioned to create work for a specific business use, such as illustrations, advertisements, and the design of books and posters.

COMMISSION, 22: (1) A work of art produced at the request of a patron. (2) The appointment of an artist to create such a work of art.

COMPOSITION, 8, 12, 18, 22, 32, 34, 44. *See also* DESIGN

CONTOUR, 16, 36, 44: An outline or the suggestion of an outline, especially of an irregular shape.

CONTRAST, 12, 20, 24, 28, 36: Big differences in light and dark, shapes, colors, and activity.

*Country Dog Gentlemen*, 41

De Forest, Roy, 40

DESIGN, 40: (1) The arrangement of objects and figures in a painting through the combination of colors and shapes. This is also called *composition*. (2) A decorative pattern of shapes, such as leaves.

DETAIL, 18, 42: (1) A small area of a painting, such as objects on a table or decorations on a dress. (2) When used in a book: a section of a painting enlarged to provide a close-up view of textures and colors.

*Dog, A*, 25

DRAWING, 10, 20, 26: The art of creating an image by making marks on paper. Drawings can be made using dry materials such as pencil, charcoal, and crayon or wet materials such as ink and paint. Drawings may consist of lines, tones, shading, and dots. Twentieth-century artists began to create drawings that are difficult to distinguish from paintings. An important difference is that drawings are usually on paper rather than canvas, wood, or metal. Drawings produced with more than one kind of material are known as mixed-media drawings.

DYNAMIC, 22, 32, 38: A term used to describe shapes that suggest motion through their directional form, such as a triangle, a sharp curve, and a slanted line.

*Flying Yellow Dog*, 45

FOREGROUND, 14, 16, 24, 30, 34, 38: The area in a painting closest to the viewer. *See also* BACKGROUND

FORM, 12, 30, 36, 38, 42: All of the qualities that uniquely describe a person or object, including size, weight, color, shape, texture, tone, and movement.

FRESCO, 8: A method of painting onto wet plaster, usually with watercolor, to create a picture in which the paint is absorbed into the wall instead of remaining on the surface. *See also* MURAL

*Gian Federico Madruzzo*, 13

GLAZE, 18: A transparent, or almost transparent, film of paint, applied over dry paint, that changes the colors underneath.

Goya y Lucientes, Francisco de, 24

*Group of Artists*, 29

HIGHLIGHT, 18, 22, 24, 38: The lightest color or brightest white in a painting.

Hopper, Edward, 34

*Hunting Scene*, 9

ILLUMINATED MANUSCRIPT, 16: A hand-painted book created by artists and artisans that also contains decorative hand-drawn lettering called calligraphy. Each illuminated manuscript is unique, unlike books that are mechanically produced on printing presses.

*In the Rain*, 31

Katz, Alex, 38

Laurencin, Marie, 28

LINE, 14, 22, 28, 30, 32, 34, 36, 42: (1) A mark, such as a pencil mark, that does not include gradual shades or tones. (2) An outline or a contour that conveys the form of an object or a person.

*Man Leading Dog*, 37

Marc, Franz, 30

Moroni, Giovanni Battista, 12

MURAL, 8, 24: A very large painting that decorates a wall or is created as part of a wall. Also called a wall painting.

North, Noah, 26

OPAQUE, 12, 18, 22: Not letting light pass through. Opaque paints conceal what is under them. (The opposite of TRANSPARENT)

PAINT: Artists have used different kinds of paint, depending on the materials that were available to them and the effects they wished to produce in their work.

Different kinds of paint are similar in the way they are made.

1. Paint is made by combining finely powdered pigment with a vehicle. A vehicle is a fluid that evenly disperses the color. The kind of vehicle used sometimes gives the paint its name, for example: oil paint.

Pigment is the raw material that gives paint its color. Pigments can be made from natural minerals and from chemical compounds.

2. Paint is made thinner or thicker with a substance called a medium, which can produce a consistency like that of water or mayonnaise or peanut butter.

3. A solvent must be used by the painter to clean the paint from brushes, tools, and the hands. The solvent must be appropriate for the composition of the paint.

ACRYLIC PAINT, 40, 44: Pigment is combined with an acrylic polymer vehicle that is created in a laboratory. By itself, acrylic paint dries rapidly. Several different mediums can be used with acrylic paint: retarders slow the drying process, flow extenders thin the paint, an impasto medium thickens the paint, a gloss medium makes it shiny, a matte medium makes it dull.

Acrylic paint has been popular since the 1960s. Many artists like its versatility and the wide range of colors available. Acrylic paint is also appreciated because its solvent is water, which is nonhazardous.

OIL PAINT, 22, 40: Pigment is combined with an oil vehicle (usually linseed or poppy oil). The medium chosen by most artists is linseed oil; the solvent is turpentine. Oil paint is never mixed with water. Oils dry slowly, enabling the artist to work on a painting for a long time. Some painters add other materials, such as pumice powder or marble dust, to produce thick layers of color. Oil paint has been used since the fifteenth century. Until the early nineteenth century, artists or their assistants ground the pigment and combined the ingredients of paint in their studios. When the flexible tin tube (like a toothpaste tube) was invented in 1840, paint made by art suppliers became available.

WATERCOLOR, 8, 16: Pigment is combined with gum arabic, a water-based vehicle. Water is both the medium and the solvent. Watercolor paint now comes ready to use in tubes (moist) or in cakes (dry). Watercolor paint is thinned with water, and areas of paper are often left uncovered to produce highlights.

*Gouache* is an opaque form of watercolor, which is also called tempera or body color.

Watercolor paint was first used 37,000 years ago by cave dwellers who created the first wall paintings.

PALETTE, 8, 34: (1) A flat tray used by a painter for laying out and mixing colors. (2) The range of colors selected by a painter for a work.

PATRON, 12, 22: An individual or organization that supports the arts or an individual artist.

PERSPECTIVE, 14, 26: Perspective is a method of representing people, places, and things in a painting or drawing to make them appear solid or three-dimensional rather than flat. Six basic rules of perspective are used in Western art.

1. People in a painting appear larger when near and gradually become smaller as they get farther away.

2. People in the foreground overlap people or objects behind them.

3. People become closer together as they get farther away.

4. People in the distance are closer to the top of the picture than those in the foreground.

5. Colors are brighter and shadows are stronger in the foreground. Colors and shadows are paler and softer in the background. This technique is often called *atmospheric perspective*.

6. Lines that in real life are parallel (such as the line of a ceiling and the line of a floor) are drawn at an angle, and the lines meet at the *horizon line*, which represents the eye level of the artist and the viewer.

In addition, a special technique of perspective, called *foreshortening*, is used to compensate for distortion in figures and objects painted on a flat surface. For example, an artist will paint the hand of an outstretched arm larger than it is in proportion to the arm, which becomes smaller as it recedes toward the shoulder. This correction, necessary in a picture using perspective, is automatically made by the human eye observing a scene in life. *Foreshortening* refers to the representation of figures or objects, whereas *perspective* refers to the representation of a scene or a space.

Painters have used these methods to depict objects in space since the fifteenth century. However, many twentieth-century artists choose not to use perspective. An artist might emphasize colors, lines, or shapes to express an idea instead of showing people or objects in a realistic space.

*Pierrepont Edward Lacey and His Dog, Gun*, 27

PLASTER, 8: A chalky white powder made of gypsum and lime. When mixed with water it forms a thick paste that dries to a hard finish.

*Plato Gives Advice to Iskandar*, 17

PORTRAIT, 10, 16, 18, 20, 22, 26, 28, 38: A painting, drawing, sculpture, or photograph that represents an individual's appearance and, usually, his or her personality.

*Portrait of an Extraordinary Musical Dog*, 23
*Prince Ferdinand VI*, 19
*Puppy Carrying a Pheasant Feather*, 11

Ranc, Jean, 18
Reinagle, Philip, 22
*Roof Playground, The*, 33

Sánchez Luján, Gilbert, 42

SCALE, 16, 24: The relationship of the size of an object to that of a human or an animal. For example, in a painting that depicts a mountain, we can judge the mountain's size only if we compare it to that of a human or an animal.

SELF-PORTRAIT, 24, 28: A painting of the artist by the artist. *See also* PORTRAIT

SHADING, 16, 18, 20, 34: The use of gradually darker and lighter colors to make an object appear solid and three-dimensional.

SHADOW, 16, 22, 24, 28, 34: An area made darker than its surroundings because direct light does not reach it.

*Stepping Out*, 43
Stubbs, George, 20
*Sunny*, 39

TEXTURE, 20, 40, 44: The surface quality of a painting. For example, an oil painting could have a thin, smooth surface texture, or a thick, rough surface texture.

TONE, 12, 20: The sensation of an overall coloration in a painting. For example, an artist might begin by painting the entire picture in shades of greenish gray. After more colors are applied using transparent glazes, shadows, and highlights, the mass of greenish gray color underneath will show through and create an even tone, or *tonal harmony*.

Painters working with opaque colors can achieve the same effect by adding one color, such as green, to every other color on their palette. This makes all of the colors seem more alike, or harmonious. The effect of tonal harmony is part of the artist's vision and begins with the first brushstrokes. It cannot be added to a finished painting. *See also* COLOR

TRANSPARENT, 12, 34: Allowing light to pass through so colors underneath can be seen. (The opposite of OPAQUE)

Traylor, Bill, 36

TURPENTINE, 12, 22: A strong-smelling solvent made from pine sap used in oil painting. (*See also* PAINT; OIL PAINT)

*White Poodle in a Punt*, 21

Yi Om, 10

Zorach, William, 32

# Credits

Frontispiece
*DOG*, 1967
Wayne Thiebaud, American
Graphite on illustration board
9⅛" x 7⅜"
Private Collection

Page
9   *HUNTING SCENE*, detail, 12th century
Unknown Spanish artist
© Museo del Prado, Madrid

10  *TWO PUPPIES*, c. 1830
I. Herring, American
Lithograph, 10" x 15"
Smithsonian Institution, Washington, D.C.
Harry T. Peters America on Stone Lithography Collection

11  *PUPPY CARRYING A PHEASANT FEATHER*, 16th century
Yi Om, Korean
Philadelphia Museum of Art, Purchased (59.105.1)

13  *GIAN FEDERICO MADRUZZO*, c. 1560
Giovanni Battista Moroni, Italian
National Gallery of Art, Washington, D.C., Timken Collection
(1960.6.27)

15  *THE ANIMALS ENTERING NOAH'S ARK*, detail
Jacopo Bassano, Italian
© Museo del Prado, Madrid

17  *PLATO GIVES ADVICE TO ISKANDAR*, detail, 1597–98
Attributed to Basawan, Indian
From a Kamseh of Amir Khusrau of Delhi
The Metropolitan Museum of Art, Gift of Alexander Smith Cochran, 1913
(13.228.30). Photograph by Schecter Lee

18  *GREYHOUND*, c. 1500
Albrecht Dürer, German (1471–1528)
Brush drawing in gray ink, 5¾" x 7¾"
Royal Collection, Windsor

19  *PRINCE FERDINAND VI*, c. 1725
Jean Ranc, French
© Museo del Prado, Madrid

20  *POMERANIAN BITCH AND PUPPY*, c. 1777
Thomas Gainsborough, English
Oil on canvas, 32½" x 43½"
National Gallery, London

21  *WHITE POODLE IN A PUNT*, c. 1780
George Stubbs, English
Courtesy Mr. Paul Mellon, Upperville, Virginia

22  *BULLDOG*, c. 1815
Théodore Géricault, French
Oil on canvas, 16⅛ x 11⅜
Musée des Beaux-Arts André Malraux, Le Havre

23  *PORTRAIT OF AN EXTRAORDINARY MUSICAL DOG*, c. 1805
Philip Reinagle, English
Virginia Museum of Fine Arts, The Paul Mellon Collection (85.465)

24  *DOG BARKING AT THE MOON*, c. 1800
Philipp Otto Runge, German
Paper cutout, 7⅞" x 4⅛"
Kunsthalle, Hamburg

25  *A DOG*, c. 1820–23
Francisco de Goya y Lucientes, Spanish
Mural transferred to canvas, 53½" x 32"
© Museo del Prado, Madrid

27  *PIERREPONT EDWARD LACEY AND HIS DOG, GUN*, c. 1835–36
Attributed to Noah North, American
Memorial Art Gallery of the University of Rochester
Gift of Ms. & Mrs. Robert Dunn. Photo: James Via (78.189.)

28  *A SHEPHERD'S DOG (BRIZO)*, 1864
Marie Rosalie "Rosa" Bonheur, French (1822–99)
Oil on canvas, 17¼" x 14¼"
Wallace Collection, London

29  *GROUP OF ARTISTS*, 1908
Marie Laurencin, French
The Baltimore Museum of Art. The Cone Collection, formed by Dr. Claribel Cone
and Miss Etta Cone of Baltimore, Maryland. (1950.215)

31  *IN THE RAIN*, 1912
Franz Marc, German
Stüdtische Galerie im Lenbachhaus, Munich

33  *THE ROOF PLAYGROUND*, detail, 1917
William Zorach, American
Whitney Museum of American Art, New York. Gift of Mr. and Mrs. Arthur G.
Altschul. Photo: Geoffrey Clements, New York (71.231.)

34  *HOUND IN A FIELD*, 1958
Alex Colville, Canadian (born 1920)
Casein tempera on board, 30" x 40"
National Gallery of Canada, Ottawa

35  *CAPE COD EVENING*, 1937
Edward Hopper, American
National Gallery of Art, Washington, D.C., John Hay Whitney Collection
(1982.76.6. PA)

37  *MAN LEADING DOG*, c. 1939–42
Bill Traylor, American
Collection Petry-Mills, Chicago
Courtesy Carl Hammer Gallery, Chicago

39  *SUNNY*, 1971
Alex Katz, American
Milwaukee Art Museum , Gift of Mrs. Harry Lynde Bradley

40  *POOCH*, c. 1937
Milton Avery, American (1885–1965)
Litho crayon, 8½" x 11"
Courtesy Grace Borgenicht Gallery, New York

41  *COUNTRY DOG GENTLEMEN*, 1973
Roy De Forest, American
San Francisco Museum of Modern Art, Gift of the Hamilton-Wells Collection

42  *DRAWING OF A DOG*,
Leonardo da Vinci, Italian (1452–1519)
Chalk on paper
Royal Collection, Windsor

43  *STEPPING OUT*, 1986
Gilbert Sánchez Luján, American
Courtesy of the artist, © Magui 1986

45  *FLYING YELLOW DOG*, 1985–93
Grimanessa Amoros, Peruvian
Courtesy of the artist